.n

Mapping Earthforms

Rivers

Catherine Chambers

Heinemann
LIBRARY

First published in Great Britain by Heinemann Library,
Halley Court, Jordan Hill, Oxford OX2 8EJ,
a division of Reed Educational and Professional Publishing Ltd.
Heinemann is a registered trademark of Reed Educational & Professional Publishing Limited.

OXFORD MELBOURNE AUCKLAND
JOHANNESBURG BLANTYRE GABORONE
IBADAN PORTSMOUTH NH (USA) CHICAGO

Designed by David Oakley
Illustrations by Tokay Interactive Ltd
Originated by Dot Gradations
Printed in Hong Kong/China

04 03 02 01 00
10 9 8 7 6 5 4 3 2 1

ISBN 0 431 09844 1

British Library Cataloguing in Publication Data

Chambers, Catherine
    Rivers. – (Mapping earthforms)
    1. Stream ecology – Juvenile literature 2. Rivers – Maps –
    Juvenile literature
    I. Title
    577.6'4

Acknowledgements
The Publishers would like to thank the following for permission to reproduce photographs: Bruce Coleman
Limited: A Potts p17; Ecoscene: R Greenwood p9, Gryniewicz p24, N Hawkes p5; Robert Harding Picture
Library: p26, C Bowman p20, E Young p6; Anthony King: p25; Minden Pictures: p13; Oxford Scientific Films: C
Lockwood, Earth Scenes p11, G Kidd p16, H and J Beste p18, K Ringland p19; Still Pictures: P Harrison p23, H
Schwarzbach p29, J Schytte p14; Tony Stone Images: p4.

Cover photograph reproduced with permission of Robert Harding Picture Library.

Every effort has been made to contact copyright holders of any material reproduced in this book. Any
omissions will be rectified in subsequent printings if notice is given to the Publisher.

For more information about Heinemann Library books, or to order, please phone ++44 (0)1865 888066, or send
a fax to ++44 (0)1865 314091. You can visit our website at www.heinemann.co.uk.

Any words appearing in the text in bold, **like this**, are explained in the Glossary.

Contents

What is a river?

A river is a body of flowing water. Sometimes it rushes and rages. At other times it flows slowly along. But a river is always pulled by the Earth's **gravity** from high ground down to a large lake or to the sea. A stream is a smaller body of water that flows into a river. We will see how a river and its streams make up a **river system**.

How did rivers begin?

Water began from gases that formed around the Earth millions of years ago. Millions of years ago, too, mountain peaks arose when great **plates** of the Earth's crust pushed together. The rain that fell on the mountains gathered in dips and cracks. It then began to flow as streams and rivers. We will find out how the Earth's **water cycle** continues to make streams and rivers flow.

The Amazon is the second-longest river in the world. It is so long that it flows through many different **climates** and types of **vegetation.** It runs from the cold Andes mountains through hot **tropical** rainforests and into the Atlantic Ocean.

What do rivers look like?

Rivers begin on higher ground as streams, springs or patches of soggy ground. As the water gathers, it flows down the mountainside – sometimes as a waterfall. As the slope flattens, the river still flows quickly. It also becomes wider. The river widens even more as it reaches a lake or the sea. Here, it slows down. The strength of the water and the pull of gravity help to carve out shapes in the Earth. We will see how rivers change the landscape and find out how rivers themselves are always changing.

Life in and around rivers

Rivers teem with life. Plants thrive in and around them. All kinds of animals live in or close to the water. Humans could not have survived without rivers. We will see how living things have adapted to them. We will also discover how humans have changed rivers and their landscapes in different parts of the world.

Plants, animals and humans cannot live without water. Clean rivers like this one provide the perfect **habitat** for many living **species**. Polluted rivers have less oxygen in the water. This harms life in the river.

Rivers of the world

The world has millions of rivers and streams. Some rivers are tiny. Others flow a very long way through huge land masses called **continents**. For example, if you look at the continent of Africa, you can see the mighty River Nile winding far down the eastern side. The River Niger cuts a curve through the west of the continent.

Rare rivers

But the world is not completely covered with rivers. There is a huge area of northern Africa where you can see no rivers at all. This is because the **climate** here is very dry. In all deserts there is very little rain. When rain does fall, it really pours down. The rainstorms make rivers in the sand and dry rock. These rivers soon disappear when the sun beats down on them and dry winds blow. Only dry river beds remain.

The Rocky Mountains stretch all the way from Mexico to Canada. Along part of it they form a **watershed** called the Great Divide. It runs from Colorado in the USA northward to Canada. The great Colorado River flows down the west side and runs through rocky desert and the Grand Canyon.

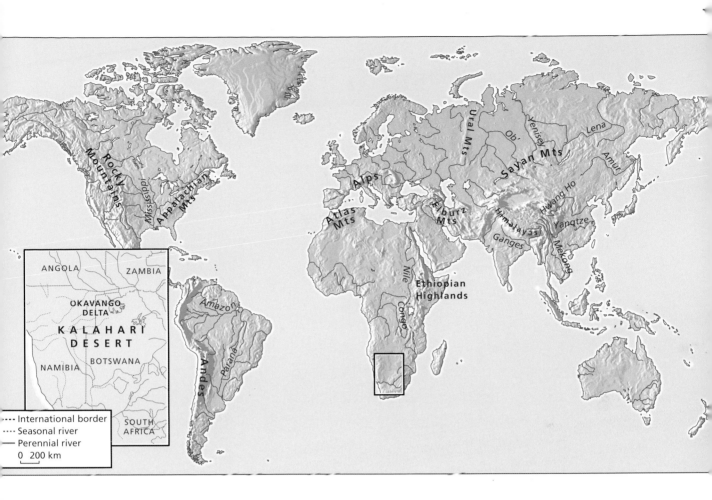

The main map shows the world's major rivers and mountain ranges. The inset shows an area of southern Africa where there are many seasonal rivers.

Some areas of the world, like Botswana, have two main seasons during the year. One is dry and the other is wet. Rivers often flow only in the wet season. These are called seasonal rivers.

Mountains, rain and rivers

Most long rivers flow from high mountains. On the map you can see many flowing down one side of the Andes in South America. This is because **trade winds** pick up moisture from the world's oceans and blow it towards the mountain range. The moisture turns into rain as it rises up the slope. The rain falls high on the mountain and flows back down to form a river. It is very dry on the other side of the mountain where the rain does not reach.

The river system

A **river system** is made up of one major river and all the streams that run down into it. It is contained in a **drainage basin.** Even if the basin is huge, it still has sloping sides. It is separated from other river basins by the high rim or ridge of ground around it. This rim is called the **watershed.**

The river system is the water that you can actually see in rivers and streams. But more water feeds the system from under the ground. It soaks, or percolates, through the earth and soft rock. The percolated water and the river system above ground are together known as the river catchment area. But how does water continually feed the rivers and streams?

This is the river system of the Mississippi River. It covers much of the USA, with **tributaries** such as the Missouri and Ohio Rivers flowing from the mountains in the west and east of the country.

The Earth's water cycle

There is always the same amount of water on Earth. But it comes in different forms. Most water fills our oceans, seas and lakes or runs in rivers and streams. Some of it soaks into the ground. Sometimes water falls as rain or it comes as melted snow and ice. At other times it is held in tiny droplets in the clouds, mist and fog. Sometimes you cannot see water at all. When it is sunny, water is

evaporated into the air – mostly from our oceans, seas and greatest lakes. It rises into the air as invisible **water vapour**. Plants let water vapour into the air through holes in their leaves too.

This water vapour often forms clouds high up. As the clouds get even higher, the water in them cools and becomes water droplets. These fall as rain. The rain then fills streams and rivers, lakes and seas. And then, when the sun beats down on these waters, the same cycle happens all over again. The **water cycle** is also known as the hydrological cycle. It is a system that affects the whole world, although some parts of the world are a lot wetter than others. Each river drainage basin has its own small water cycle too.

The amount of water that you can see on the Earth changes all the time. In summer, the sun evaporates a lot of water. This leaves low rivers and lakes — or even no rivers and lakes! In winter there is more rain and the rivers fill and flow.

From the mountains to the sea

A river begins high up at its **source**. The source can be mountain springs that bubble up and flow down a mountain's steep sides. It can also be small streams, formed by rain-water, that trickle over the steep rock. Some rivers begin as mountain marshes, or rain-water seeping through sponge-like rock.

The water at the source of the river is pulled down the mountain slope by the Earth's **gravity**. It carries on until it reaches a lake or the sea. This point is called the river's mouth. The journey between the source and the mouth is its course. More water is added to the river by streams known as **tributaries**.

As the river flows along its course it carves out a channel. So do all the tributaries that feed the river. Gravity tries to pull the river down in a straight line. But the waters find all sorts of obstacles in their way. It is these obstacles that help make the curved shapes of our river landscapes.

Making the channel

Earth and rock is worn away as the river flows over it, carving out the channel. This process is called **erosion**. Some of the erosion is made by the water itself. But some is made by the bits of rock and soil that get carried along in the flowing water. This rock and soil is called the river's load. The load bumps and scrapes along the channel, wearing it away. This kind of erosion is known as **corrasion**.

Rivers also carry chemicals in them. Some of these chemicals dissolve soft rock. This type of erosion is called **corrosion**. Corrasion and corrosion often act together to wear away a river's course.

A third type of erosion is **attrition**, which is when the rocks and stones on the river bed crash against each other. This breaks the rocks and stones into even smaller pieces.

Changing the channel

Erosion changes the shape and depth of the river's channel all the time. So does **deposition**. This is when the river drops, or deposits, its load of rocks and soil along the way. Mostly, deposition occurs when there has been heavy rainfall or a flood of water from ice that has thawed higher up in the river's course. At these times the river is full and fast-flowing – it carries a lot of eroded material with it. The river drops large rocks and boulders first, quite high up in its course. As the course flattens, the river sheds smaller stones. When it reaches the sea the river deposits fine soil called **silt**.

The mouth of the Mississippi opens into the Gulf of Mexico. Here the river splits into **bayous**. They are marshy outlets where the water forces itself through the silty deposits. The Mississippi deposits over 300 million cubic metres of silt every year.

River landscapes

Rivers **erode** and deposit material all the time. This is because they are finding the easiest, smoothest way towards the sea.

The river profile

The side view of a person's face is called the profile. The diagram below shows the profile of a river as it runs its course. The top line of this side view is very bumpy. This is because the river has worn away soft rock but cannot wear away the hard rock that gets in its way. Water now has to cascade over a hard edge as a waterfall. It then has to fill a lake before it trickles over the rocky lip and down towards the sea.

The bottom line shows what the river is trying to do. It is trying to wear away a totally smooth profile. This would give the river an easy journey to its mouth.

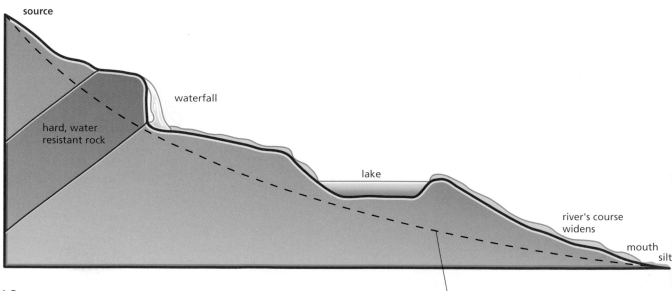

source

hard, water resistant rock

waterfall

lake

river's course widens

mouth
silt

The river is trying to erode a straight flat course, like this.

Shapes in the course

As the river leaves the mountain it reaches the valley floor, which it has helped to carve out itself. Here it **scours** out its channel in the softest rock. It often flows quickly as rapids over bands and outcrops of hard rock. The river drops some of its load as it flows.

Further along, the valley floor gets flatter and the river gets a bit slower. This part is called the river **flood plain**. Here, even more of the load is dumped. The relentless water struggles to move through the river's deposits. The river moves in curves around the deposits and hard rock. These curves are called **meanders**. Rivers make many different shapes in the earth and rock.

When the neck of a meander gets very narrow, the river water begins to flow straight over it. The loop gets cut off, leaving a lake called a cut-off or an oxbow.

Where the river meets the sea

When the river joins the sea it flows very slowly, and its load of fine **silt** finally sinks. The sluggish water has to make its way around these deposits. As it does so, it splits up into streams called **distributaries**. This low-lying plain of distributaries and silt is called a **delta**. Sometimes, islands are formed where distributaries flow around a large bank of silt.

The mighty Nile

The River Nile is the longest river in the world. It flows along the east side of Africa for 6670 kilometres (4140 miles). Its **source** springs from the Ruwenzori mountain range in Tanzania. The river flows from Lake Victoria northwards until it reaches Egypt and the Mediterranean Sea. The Nile has made huge features in the landscape all along its course. It flows through different types of **climate** and **vegetation**.

The course of the Nile

The river profile on page 12 shows a simple course. There is just one waterfall and one lake as the river makes its way to the sea.

Many different types of boat sail along the wide, deep parts of the River Nile. These small trading vessels are called feluccas.

You can see from the map that the Nile has a long, complicated course. There are many **tributary** rivers, waterfalls and lakes. There are long stretches of turbulent waters that run over huge boulders in the river channel. These stretches are called **cataracts**. The river flows into lakes and then out of them again. It passes through a great swamp known as the Sudd. The Nile has thousands of small **meanders**. It also has two huge bends that pass through the Nubian Desert.

Different climates

The Nile is so long that it flows through different climates. Like most rivers, the Nile has a high, cool source in the mountains. The Nile then passes through forests which are warm and wet until it reaches the **flood plain**, where the temperatures are very hot and dry. At the coast, there are cool, wet winters and hot, dry summers, which together are known as a Mediterranean **climate**.

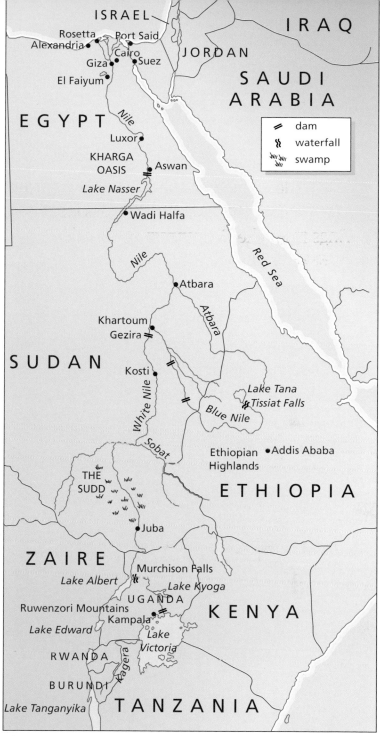

The map shows **dams** that were made by people. These have been designed to help humans to use the river. People have also stopped some of the waterfalls to make the course smoother.

River plants

Where river plants grow

Flowing water is known as a **lotic habitat** for both plants and animals. Many plants have adapted well to living in it. But large river plants do not grow easily near cold mountain waterfalls. They cannot grow well in shallow, fast-flowing stretches of rivers with stony beds either. Here, mosses and tiny **algae** grow best because they hug the rocks. Algae are the simplest form of plant life. They have a jelly-like coating which reduces the rubbing action, or friction, of the flowing water. Small mosses cling on with grips that grow in line with the flowing **current.** This stops the water from pressing hard against them and tearing the mosses away from the rocks.

◈ The bulrush is a member of the reed-mace family. It grows in shallow fresh water in many parts of the world. Bulrushes grow between 1.5 and 2.5 m tall. This helps them to cope when river waters rise. The stem is strong, with a waxy coating to protect it from the water. The flowers are tiny and tightly packed into a long plume. Leaves are wide, waxy and very tough. They receive a lot of moisture drawn up from the roots of the plants. But this is **evaporated** through tiny holes in the leaves. The leaves of bulrushes can be woven and made into baskets. The fleshy pulp inside the stem is dried and made into rope.

Along the warmer **flood plain** the river bed often has a lot of very fine, deep, rich soil. So do the marshes that spread out from the river itself. Here, many larger plants have been able to adapt to life in and around the water. These still or slower-flowing waters are known as **lentic** habitats.

The water hyacinth comes from South America but has now spread to North America and Australia. It has blue flowers with yellow spots. These form a spike set high above the water. The leaf-stalks have many air pockets. They help the plant to float well above the surface. The stems are strong to cope with the flowing water. They have many fibres. The fibres can be made into paper or dried and used for fuel. The water hyacinth is also known as the million-dollar weed. This is because it has cost millions of dollars to stop it from clogging the **river systems** in the southern USA!

River animals

Rivers teem with many kinds of **mammals, amphibians, reptiles,** birds, fish and insects. Most **species** live in the calmer waters of the **flood plain** and marshlands. But others have adapted to fast-flowing waters higher up the river's course. They have developed streamlined bodies which reduce the impact of the rushing water. The **larvae** of blackfly have even got hooks and suckers so that they can attach themselves firmly to the rocks.

Living in the river

Mammals such as beavers have developed webbed feet to help them swim in the water. So have amphibians, such as frogs, and waterbirds, like ducks. Crocodiles are reptiles that swim by swinging their long powerful tails from side to side.

What is this amazing creature with a duck's bill, webbed feet, a furry body and a squashed tail? It is in fact a mammal called the duck-billed platypus. The platypus lives in southern Australia and Tasmania. The female digs burrows in the river bank. She lays her eggs in a nest made of weeds, leaves and grasses. The platypus uses its flat tail and webbed feet to swim. The long bill stirs up the mud at the bottom of the river. This uncovers the platypus's food of insects, worms and shellfish.

River mammals can hold their breath for a long time underwater. This is so that they can find their food. Amphibians filter oxygen in the water through their skin. The skin is thin, with a lot of blood near the surface. This is so that oxygen gets taken into the blood stream very quickly. They can also breathe when they are out of the water. Fish use gills at the side of their heads as well as their skin. Reptiles stay in the water for a long time. But they breathe in air above the water.

Most river creatures use their large mouths to catch their prey or bite off river plants. But the crocodile swims quietly to shallow water. Here, it snatches its victims with its tail. Then the crocodile drags the prey into deep water. But the crocodile does not eat all the time. When it is very hot or very cold the crocodile buries itself in wet mud by the river's edge. Here it sleeps for several weeks.

The Atlantic salmon lives in parts of the Atlantic Ocean until it is time to breed. Then it swims upriver, leaping up fast-flowing rapids using its strong muscles. Then the female makes a nest in the stony bed of a mountain stream. She lays as many as 20,000 eggs and protects them with stones and **silt**. The adult fish then let the river **current** take them back down to the sea. The young salmon hatch and stay in the river for about two years. Then they go down to the sea until it is time for them to breed.

Living with the river

For thousands of years rivers have provided drinking water, food and well-watered farmland. Riverside plants have been used as materials for building homes both in and around the water.

Boats have been made from river reeds, wood and tree bark. The waters have given people a way of transporting goods and people to other settlements.

Rivers have protected people against their enemies. Many old towns and villages were built where a **tributary** joins the main river. This was even better for protection and transport. Some ancient settlements were built inside the loop of a **meander**. This meant that only one wall needed to be built to protect the community. Many rivers also provide a natural border between countries, such as the Rio Grande which marks the border between Texas in the USA and Mexico. Rivers are so important to the world that they have become part of religion for many peoples.

Steamboats helped the river port of New Orleans to grow. This great city curves around a bend in a wide part of the Mississippi River. Ships can sail from here to the Atlantic Ocean along channels that have been **dredged** to make them deeper. The settlement was at first a group of Native American villages. Over 200 years ago New Orleans began to **export** crops such as cotton to other parts of the world. Now it exports oil products too.

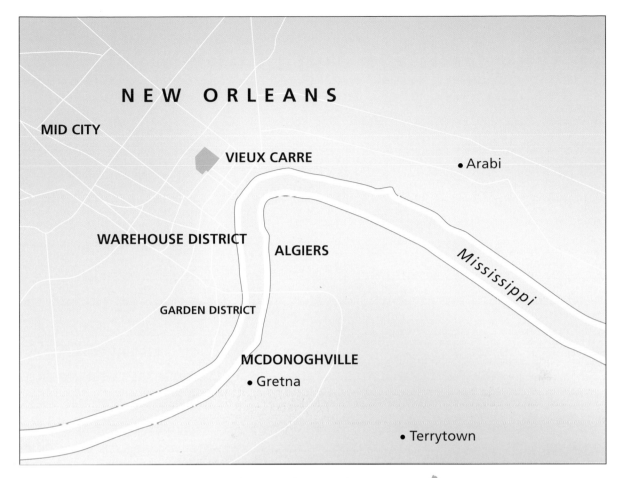

But rivers can also bring problems for settlements, such as flooding. Diseases such as malaria are also more widespread near wet or damp areas.

Cities and civilizations

Some of the greatest cities of the world began as small settlements where the river flows deep and wide. Large boats brought goods and people to the city. This allowed trade to develop. Later, factories were built in cities near the river. Here, the factory owners used **raw materials**, such as cotton, brought by ships. The raw materials were then manufactured into goods.

Great civilizations also developed on the banks of rivers. Ancient Egypt grew on the banks of the River Nile over 5000 years ago.

The oldest areas of New Orleans, such as the Vieux Carre or French Quarter, were built around a sharp bend in the Mississippi River. New Orleans now covers a much larger area, including Algiers, on the inside of the meander.

A way of life – Bangladesh

Most of Bangladesh lies where the great Ganges and Brahmaputra Rivers meet the sea. In this **delta** area, the land is very flat and low lying. During the cool, dry months the rivers fork out into **distributaries.** These make their way out into the Indian Ocean. But during the summer months rain pours down and water flows from the melting snows in the great Himalayan mountain range.

The river delta is flooded with a stretch of water that covers many square kilometres. Sometimes storm surges create huge waves

This map shows Bangladesh during the dry winter months. The rivers are still flowing inside their normal banks. The map would look very different in the summer. Then, there are about 5080 mm of rain in the north-east, and 1400 mm in the east-central region. This floods the delta. The darker areas of the map are very low lying.

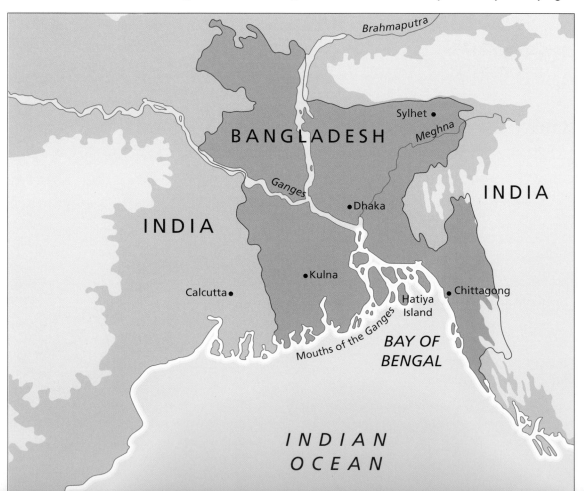

which smother the delta in sea-water too. The flood-waters kill many of the plants beneath them. But billions of tiny blue-green **algae** feed on the dead plants and create lots of nitrogen in the soil. This makes the land very **fertile** and good for farming.

Jute is grown where the farmland floods. Its stems are woody and have many fibres. These are soaked, dried and made into rope, sacking and matting.

Living and working in Bangladesh

The people living on the delta always have to be prepared for flooding. They build their homes on banks or platforms of earth. The houses are mostly made of wood and are set on stilts. Even so, flooding often causes a lot of deaths, and damage to farmland.

In the dry winters the ground is full of large holes. This is where the earth was dug up to make the banks and platforms. The holes are called borrow pits. Water fills the pits and is used for drinking and washing. It is also used for **irrigating** crops.

Most people in Bangladesh are farmers. Two or three crops of rice are grown every year in the rich, damp soil. **Tropical** fruits, beans, oilseeds, wheat, vegetables, bamboo and jute are grown on the rest. Nearly a million tonnes of fish are caught every year. Most are fresh-water fish.

A lot of the country's electricity comes from oil and coal-fired power stations but some comes from water. This is called hydro-electric power (HEP).

Our changing rivers

Rivers change naturally all the time. As we have seen, but the way humans use rivers changes them too.

Natural flooding?

Flooding happens all the time. It occurs when there is a lot of melting snow and ice or when there is very heavy rainfall. After the flood, the river channel will have changed.

Over the last few years flooding has increased. One of the worst floods was on the River Yangtze in China, in 1998. Many people lost their lives and homes. But what has made the floods so bad? People are partly to blame.

The waterwheel is an ancient form of irrigation. This one in southern Germany picks up water in the buckets and tips it into the wooden channel, which leads to the fields.

Taking the water – changing the flow

Humans have made some of the greatest changes to rivers. One of the most important has been building **dams**. Dams are mostly built on rivers to store water and to direct it on to dry farmland. There are other types of river **irrigation**. Some use water straight from the river. This changes the way the river **erodes** its channel and deposits material.

Thousands of years ago, river irrigation was used in ancient Egypt, Mesopotamia, China and Peru. Early Native Americans irrigated more than 1000 square kilometres (380 square miles) of land in Arizona's Salt River valley.

The Riano reservoir was made to irrigate farmland and to provide power. But the old town of Riano had to be moved from the **fertile** valley floor to the bare mountainside.

Changing times

Today, boats can still sail from the Atlantic Ocean up the River Guadalquivir to the city of Seville. This is a distance of 80 kilometres (50 miles). But long ago, boats were able to reach the city port of Cordoba. This is a further 100 kilometres (75 miles) beyond Seville. Over time, the river channel filled with **silt**. This silting caused the Donana marshlands, now home to many **species** of marshland birds and animals.

Looking to the future

Dam-building, flooding and pollution are upsetting **river systems** throughout the world. Most of these problems are made by humans. We use too much water in our homes and industry – and too much energy. We pollute the rain and the rivers. The future of our rivers depends a lot on us.

The problem of dams

Dams have been built for **irrigation** and to help rivers flow all year round. They also provide hydro-electric power (HEP). The cascading water let out through the dam wall turns **turbines** which provide electricity.

But dams can flood villages and river landscapes. They stop the natural flow of rivers. This dries up river systems and destroys the **habitat** of river wildlife.

Flooding

Floods kill people and destroy homes and farmland. They also alter river channels and systems. Floods have become worse in the last few years. This is partly because storms have become more frequent and more violent.

Many scientists blame this on the world's slightly hotter weather. The increased heat **evaporates** more moisture, which turns into more rain clouds.

Some scientists think the hotter weather is caused by too many harmful gases going up into the atmosphere. These have thinned the layer of ozone gases which protects us from the sun's heat. Other harmful gases may also be responsible for hotter weather. These come from factories and cars. All these things disrupt the **water cycle**, meaning that our rivers are affected in turn.

Polluting the rivers with chemicals harms the river habitat. Chemicals from factories kill river plants. These plants root into the soils on the river bed and the river bank, holding them together. Without them, the soil is easily washed away. River plants also put oxygen into the water which is needed by fish. Farm **fertilizers** get washed down into rivers too. They make water weeds grow fast and spread rapidly.

River facts

The world's longest rivers

These are the twelve longest rivers of the world. The table shows how long the rivers are. But it does not show how much water drains into each river. Neither does it show how much water flows out through the river's mouth. This is very difficult to calculate. But it is thought that about 1600 million tonnes of water are discharged from the Mississippi into the Gulf of Mexico every day.

	Continent	Length
Nile	Africa	6670 km (4140 mi)
Amazon	South America	6450 km (4010 mi)
Yangtze	Asia	6380 km (3960 mi)
Mississippi-Missouri	North America	6020 km (3740 mi)
Yenisey-Angara	Asia	5550 km (3445 mi)
Hwang Ho	Asia	5464 km (3395 mi)
Ob-Irtysh	Asia	5410 km (3360 mi)
Congo	Africa	4670 km (2900 mi)
Mekong	Asia	4500 km (2795 mi)
Parana-Plate	South America	4500 km (2795 mi)
Amur	Asia	4400 km (2730 mi)
Lena	Asia	4400 km (2730 mi)

... and the shortest

The shortest river with a name is the Roe River in Montana, USA. It is only 61 m long!

Did you know that the Mississippi Delta is expanding every year by about 100 metres?

The River Ganges is a holy river for followers of the Hindu religion. Here, people are bathing in the waters at sunrise. This is part of their daily prayer. When a person dies their ashes, and flowers, are sprinkled on the river.

Polluted rivers

The Cuyahoga River in Ohio, USA, became so polluted that, in 1952 and again in 1969, it actually caught fire! Since then, great efforts have been made to clean up our polluted rivers.

Glossary

algae simple form of plant life, ranging from a single cell to a huge seaweed

amphibian animal, with a backbone, that develops in water and can stay in the water for long periods, but can also live on land, Frogs, toads and newts are amphibians.

attrition erosion caused by friction, or gradual wearing away

bayou marshy stream that forces itself through silt at the river's mouth

cataract waterfall or series of waterfalls

climate rainfall, temperature and winds that normally affect a large area

continent the world's largest land masses. Continents are usually divided into many countries.

corrasion when stones get carried along by flowing water and bump against the river's bed and sides, eroding them away

corrosion when something is gradually eaten away, for example through being dissolved by chemicals

current strong surge of water that flows constantly in one direction in an ocean

dam wall that is built across a river valley to hold back water, creating an artificial lake behind it

delta where a river meets the ocean and the water splits into little streams that dribble into the sea

deposition when a river drops its load of rock and silt on the river bed

distributary one of the streams a river separates into when it reaches its delta

drainage basin basin-shaped area of the Earth, surrounded by a watershed, in which a river and its tributaries flow

dredge dig out layers of silt on a river bed

erosion wearing away of rocks and soil by wind, water, ice or acid

evaporate turn from solid or liquid into vapour, such as when water becomes water vapour

export sell goods to another country

fertile rich soil in which crops can grow easily. If you fertilize something you make it fertile.

fertilizer substance added to soil to make plants grow better

flood plain flat land in a valley bottom that is regularly flooded

gravity force that causes objects to fall towards the Earth. We are all attracted to the Earth by gravity.

habitat place where a plant or animal usually grows or lives

irrigate supply a place or area with water, for example to grow crops

larva(e) the undeveloped but active young of creatures such as insects and frogs

lentic slow-moving water habitat for creatures and plants

lotic habitat of running water for plants and creatures

mammal animal that feeds its young with its own milk

meander loop in a river's course

plate area of the Earth's crust separated from other plates by deep cracks. Earthquakes, volcanic activity and the forming of mountains take place at the junctions between these plates.

raw materials natural materials that can be made into other things, such as cloth from cotton and furniture from wood. Cotton and wood are both raw materials.

reptile cold-blooded, egg-laying animal with a spine and a scaly skin, such as a crocodile

river system river and all the streams (tributaries) that run into it

scour rub hard against something, wearing it away

silt fine particles of eroded rock and soil that can settle in lakes and rivers, sometimes blocking the movement of water

source where a river begins

species one of the groups used for classifying animals. The members of each species are very similar.

trade winds winds that blow steadily towards the Equator but which get pulled westward by the rotation of the Earth

tributary stream or river that runs into a main river

tropical in or from the Tropics, which is the region between the Tropic of Cancer and the Tropic of Capricorn. These are two imaginary lines drawn around the Earth, above and below the Equator.

turbine revolving motor which is pushed around by water or steam and can produce electricity

vegetation the plants that grow in a certain area

water cycle the system by which the Earth's water is constantly changing, from rivers, lakes and seas to water vapour in the air, which falls as rain on to the ground and drains into rivers, lakes and seas again

watershed area of high ground surrounding a river's drainage basin

water vapour water that has been heated so much that it forms a gas which is held in the air – drops of water form again when the vapour is cooled. There is always water vapour present in the air.

Index